Date: 6/29/18

J 955 MAR
Markovics, Joyce L.,
Iran /

Iran

by Joyce Markovics

Consultant: Karla Ruiz, MA
Teachers College, Columbia University
New York, New York

BEARPORT
PUBLISHING

New York, New York

Credits

Cover, © Aleksander Todorovic/Shutterstock and © Anna Omelchenko/Shutterstock; TOC, © Murat Sen/iStock; 4, © Leonid Andronov/Shutterstock; 5A, © Zurijeta/Shutterstock; 5B, © Alexander Mazurkevich/Shutterstock; 7, © Borna_Mirahmadian/Shutterstock; 8, © seyediman/iStock; 9, © JTB MEDIA CREATION, Inc./Alamy; 9B, © Vladimir Wrangel/Shutterstock; 10–11, © Leonid Andronov/Shutterstock; 12, © Dani Salvá/VWPics/Alamy; 13T, © Jorge Tutor/Alamy; 13B, © Oleksandr Rupeta/Alamy; 14, © Louvre, Paris, France/Bridgeman Images; 15, © Matyas Rehak/Shutterstock; 16–17, © BornaMir/iStock; 17R, © dbimages/Alamy; 18T, © Alis Photo/Shutterstock; 18B, © Thomas_Zsebok_Images/iStock; 19, © Public Domain; 20–21, © Marcin Szymczak/Shutterstock; 21R, © Vladimir Melnik/Dreamstime; 22, © ImageBROKER/Alamy; 23, © Stuart Kelly/Alamy; 24, © FOOD/Alamy; 25, © Slavica Stajic/Shutterstock; 26–27, © PhilipCacka/iStock; 27R, © Richard Ashworth/AGE Fotostock; 28, © Mansoreh/Shutterstock; 29, © epa european pressphoto agency b.v./Alamy; 30T, © homydesign/Shutterstock and © Anton_Ivanov/Shutterstock; 30B, © Don Pablo/Shutterstock; 31 (T to B), © Martchan/Shutterstock, © thomas koch/Shutterstock, © Borna_Mirahmadian/Shutterstock, © oxine/Shutterstock, and © hlphoto/Shutterstock; 32, © LindaMarieCaldwell/iStock.

Publisher: Kenn Goin
Senior Editor: Joyce Tavolacci
Creative Director: Spencer Brinker
Design: Debrah Kaiser
Photo Researcher: Thomas Persano

Library of Congress Cataloging-in-Publication Data in process at time of publication (2017)
Library of Congress Control Number: 2016038807
ISBN-13: 978-1-68402-057-7

For more information, write to Bearport Publishing Company, Inc., 45 West 21st Street, Suite 3B, New York, New York 10010. Printed in the United States of America.

10 9 8 7 6 5 4 3 2 1

Contents

This Is Iran............. 4

Fast Facts.................30

Glossary 31

Index 32

Read More 32

Learn More Online 32

About the Author 32

ANCIENT

Beautiful

Rugged

Iran (ee-RAHN) is a country in Asia.
More than 80 million people live there.

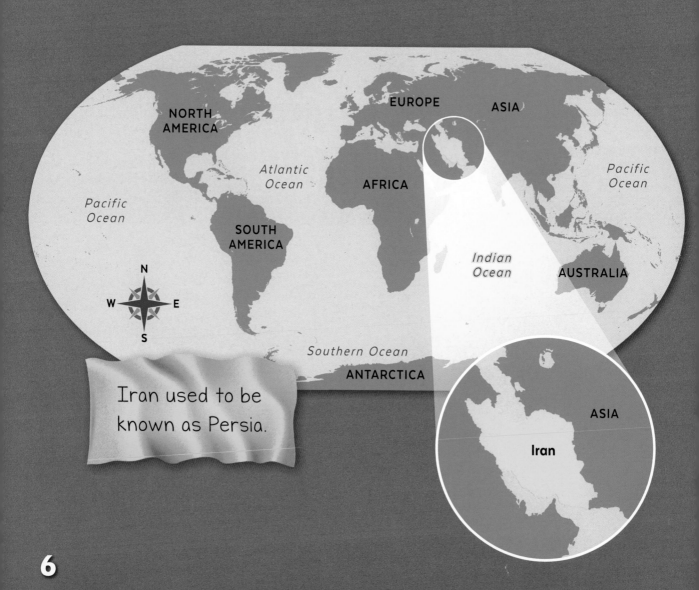

Iran used to be known as Persia.

Iran's land is varied and beautiful.

There are huge deserts.

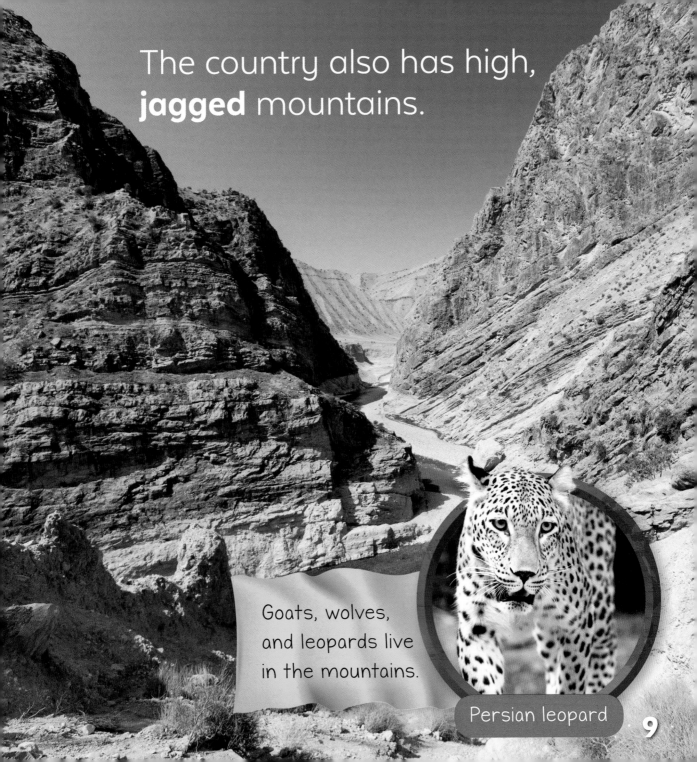

The country also has high, **jagged** mountains.

Goats, wolves, and leopards live in the mountains.

Persian leopard

9

Most people live in the central part of Iran.

This is where the country's biggest city is.

The city, called Tehran, sits at
the base of the Elburz Mountains.

Elburz Mountains

Tehran is also the
capital of Iran.

11

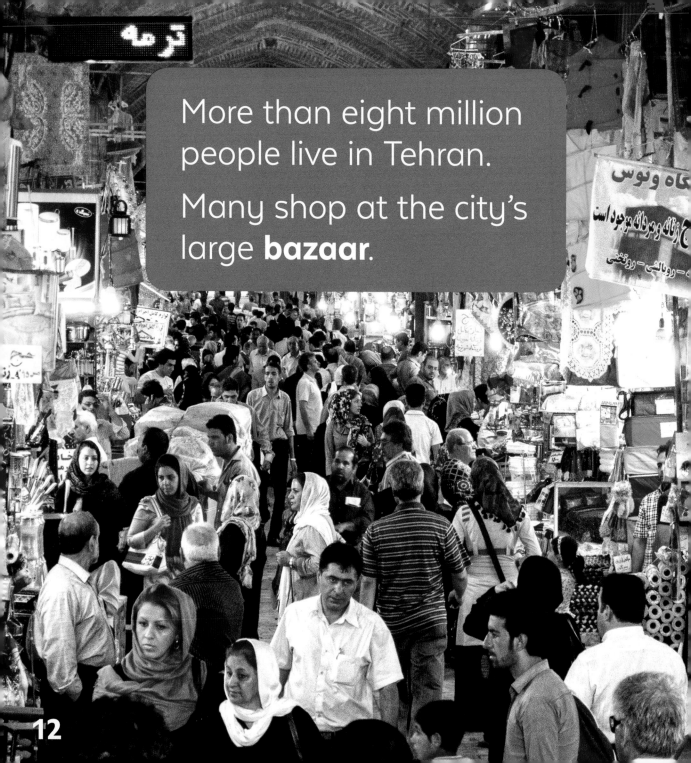

More than eight million people live in Tehran.

Many shop at the city's large **bazaar**.

The bazaar has thousands of small stores.

Shoppers can buy almost anything there!

Shopkeepers sell everything from food to jewelry to yarn and rugs.

Iran is one of the oldest countries in the world.

People have been living there for tens of thousands of years.

Ancient Iranians built big cities. Susa is one of the oldest.

an ancient structure near Susa

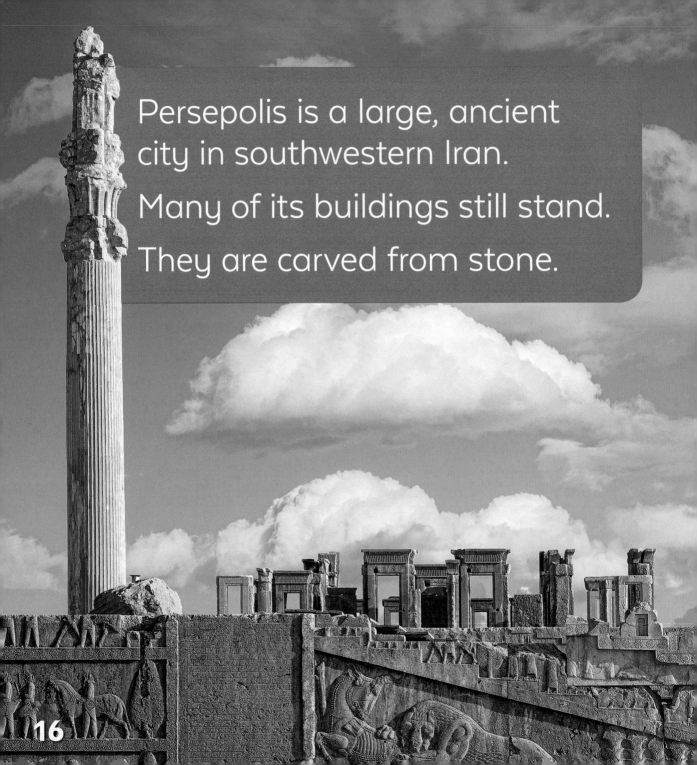

Persepolis is a large, ancient city in southwestern Iran.

Many of its buildings still stand.

They are carved from stone.

The buildings are covered with beautiful art.

Thousands of people visit Persepolis each year.

Lots of important things come from Iran.

Long ago, bricks → were **invented** there.

windmill

Ice cream and windmills come from Iran, too!

The game of polo was invented in Iran. It's played on horseback!

19

Religion is a very important part of life in Iran.

Most Iranians are Muslim.

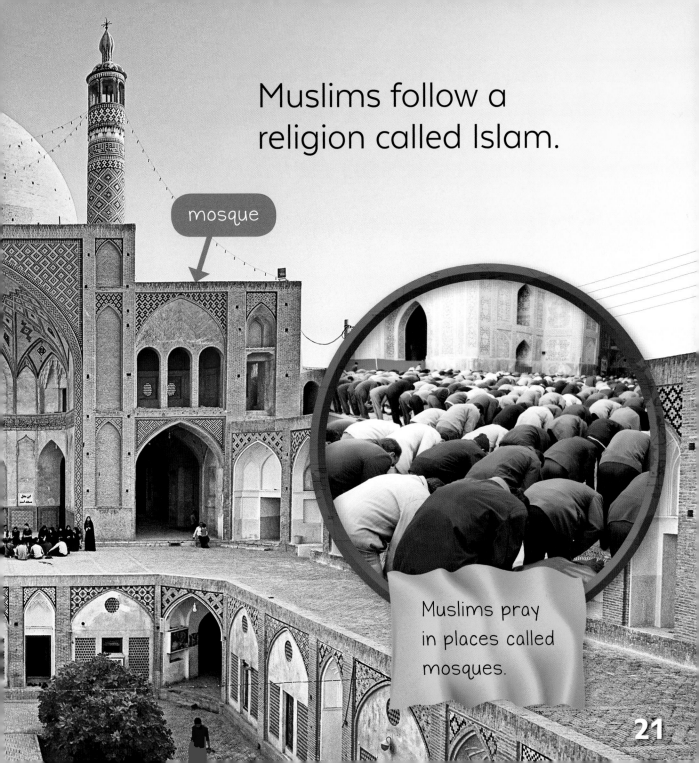

Muslims follow a religion called Islam.

mosque

Muslims pray in places called mosques.

The main language in Iran is Farsi, or Persian.

This is how you say *hello*:

Salam (sah-LAHM)

This is how you say *please*:

Lotfan (lot-FAHN)

The Persian alphabet has 32 letters.

ا ب پ ت ث ج چ ح خ د ذ

غ ع ظ ط ض ص ش س ژ ز ر

ف ق ک گ ل م ن و ه ی

خیام
Khayam

پل مارنان
Marnan Br.

خیابان شهید دکتر بهشتی
Shahid Dr. Beheshti St.

What are some tasty foods in Iran?

People enjoy grilled meat **kebabs**.

Seasoned rice is also popular.

For dessert, rose-flavored ice cream is a favorite!

What else is special about Iran?

Persian rugs!

These colorful rugs are made by hand.

The finest rugs can take 20,000 hours to complete!

Persian rugs were first made about 2,000 years ago.

Iranians celebrate many holidays.

One of the biggest is Nowruz
(no-ROOZ).

It marks the Persian New Year.

People decorate their tables
with special foods
and objects.

Nowruz means
"New Day" in Farsi.
It takes place in
late March.

a table set for Nowruz

29

Fast Facts

Capital city: Tehran

Population of Iran:
More than 80 million

Main language:
Farsi (Persian)

Money: Rial

Major religion: Islam

Nearby countries include:
Iraq, Turkey, Afghanistan, Pakistan,
Azerbaijan, Turkmenistan, and Armenia

Cool Fact: Iran is the largest grower of pistachio nuts in the world!

ancient (AYN-shunt) from a long time ago

bazaar (buh-ZAHR) a marketplace

capital (KAP-uh-tuhl) a city where a country's government is based

invented (in-VEN-tuhd) created by people

jagged (JAG-id) rough and uneven

kebabs (kuh-BOBS) small pieces of food cooked on skewers or sticks

31

Index

animals 9
art 17
capital 11, 30
cities 7, 10–11, 12,
    15, 16–17

food 24–25, 30
history 14–15, 16–17
holidays 28–29
inventions 18–19
land 8–9, 11

language 22–23,
    30
population 6, 12,
    30
religion 20–21, 30

Read More

Habeeb, William Mark.
*Iran (Major Muslim
Nations).* Broomall, PA:
Mason Crest (2010).

Simmons, Walter. *Iran
(Blastoff! Readers: Exploring
Countries).* Minnetonka, MN:
Bellwether Media (2011).

Learn More Online

To learn more about Iran, visit
www.bearportpublishing.com/CountriesWeComeFrom

About the Author

Joyce Markovics lives along the Hudson River
in a very old house. She'd like to wander
around the ruins of Persepolis one day.